based on actual events

for river
tekae
isabella
keyndyn
vic
and
d.j.

because she said "you should write a children's book about mork"

and so
of course
and also
for mork

I began my writings in the winter when the nights were cold and my hair was long

Like
seriously long.
I was practically
a woolly mammoth.
It was really
pretty
long.

I used to sleep
on the street
but now I
live in a
house.
GRR
GRR
GRR
GRR
GRR
GR
It's pretty chill here
unless you walk by...

RUFF RUFF RUFF RUFF RUFF RUFF RUFF RUFF
Then it gets the opposite of
chill. Then it gets serious.

I speak four languages.

(I can be very scary)

TAIL WAG and
PLEADING
BROWN
EYES.
SWOOSH
SWOOSH
SWOOSH
I am a master at
PLEADING BROWN EYES.
(A master.)

This move here I call HEAD TILT. This gets me lots of treats so I do this often.

My favorite treats are
CARROTS
APPLES
WATERMELON
BERRIES
PEANUT BUTTER
peanut butter
AND
BONES.

Oh,
and
anything
I
find
in
the
street.

I don't believe in the 5 second rule. I believe in the 580 millionth Kabillionth Jillionth second rule!

I also believe in finders

Keepers.

I can chase my own tail,

fly like an eagle,

and
dig
holes
all
the way
to
China!

Are we there yet?

Sometimes I
pretend I am
a lion stalking
it's prey.

And sometimes
I pretend
I am a lion
taking a nap
in the Serengeti.

The beach is my happy place.

The bathtub is not but I tolerate it okay.

I don't believe
I should ever
be on the
other side
of a
closed
door.

Like ever.

really
Like really ever.

Just
sayin.

I am an excellent companion
and if I love you I will
lick your face off!

But not right now. Right now I gotta chew on this stick.

The
End

At least for now. I
might write more
later but for now
this is The End.

xoxo

Taking a break
from his literary
pursuits the
author plays
with his big
red ball.

A. Morkus Dog a.k.a. "Mork" is a rescue from the streets of Los Angeles. He currently resides in Venice Beach where he pursues his other passions of digging, chewing, sniffing, napping, chasing, barking, licking and generally getting sand all over the place.

ISBN 978-0-578-15365-0
90000>
9 780578 153650

Made in the USA
San Bernardino, CA
06 November 2015